Poetry in Motion

A collection of poems by

James Millar

Copyright © 2014 James Millar

All rights reserved.

ISBN:1500174823
ISBN-13:9781500174828

DEDICATION

For my wife, children and grandchildren.

Poetry in Motion

Introduction

This seemed an apt name for my collection as many of the poems in the early part of the book were written on trains and other forms of public transport en route or on my way home from many of the conferences and meetings which I attended in the UK and abroad as part of my working life.

They reflected very much my mood at the time and were an invaluable way of passing the time on these long journeys.

Others were written in various places and at various times including hotel rooms in cities where often I knew no one and where television was the only other diversion.

All of this gave me the chance to gather my thoughts and to put these down on paper, something I may not have done otherwise.

I have also included a substantial number of poems which were written in more recent times which along with the others I hope you will enjoy.

CONTENTS

1 *The Train Journey*

2 *The Ticket Collector*

3 *Planning Ahead*

4 *Far From Home*

5 *The Concert*

6 *One More Night*

7 *On Stage*

8 *I Am A Singer*

9 *Dreams*

10 *Lost Love*

11 *Green Fields*

12 *An Evening Walk*

13 *Relax*

14 *Daydream*

15 *Holidays*

16 *We've Won the Cup*

17 *We are but a Song*

18 *Two Worlds*

19 *Another Day*

20 *Rhyme or Reason*

21 *Play with Words*

22 *Broken Dream*

23 *A Taste of Italy*

24 *La Belle France*

25 *Crème Brulée*

26 *The People's Choice*

27 *The woman she longed to be*

28 *Their Rock in Life*

29 *In times of need*

30 *Time to call it a day*

31 *To rhyme or not to rhyme*

ACKNOWLEDGEMENTS

*Special thanks to fellow author **Jack McGenily** for all his help and encouragement in getting this book off the ground. I wouldn't have known where to start without him and it's very much appreciated.*

Jack's books including his autobiography and children's stories can all be found on Amazon.

James Millar

The Train Journey

I sit there cramped up at a table for four

amid beer cans and magazines and bags on the floor.

I try to stretch out but just can't find a space

and I'm sure the frustration shows on my face.

The sun beats through the window and stifles the air

of the carriage which burns in the frightening glare

most people say nothing, read their books or such sit

with their eyes fixed ahead on what I know not.

Outside of the window the landscape spreads out

sleepy villages speed by with real people no doubt

what a mind numbing journey and some call this fun

I can't understand it of them I'm not one.

I sigh and sit back once again in my seat

knocking over a bag which was down at my feet.

Some people accuse me with a flash of their eyes

well at least they are human I think with surprise.

I feel like I've been on this train all my life

but at least it's "No Smoking" so I guess I'll survive.

I count off the stations as they slowly slip by

but they all look the same to my disinterested eye.

Just ten miles to go and I'll get off the train

and when the sun has gone down I'll be back home again.

As my station approaches I gather my case

my clothes are all crumpled, I fasten my lace.

The train grinds to a stop and I open the door

the fresh air's delicious, I can't wait for more.

I watch as the train disappears in the night,

and make my way home –oh what a delight.

The Ticket Collector.

Not much further to go, but what can I do

it's too late to nap, I'd just sleep right through.

The carriage is empty, the rest have all gone

but here comes the guard checking tickets for one?

He strides down the aisle probably glad that it's quiet

no drunks to climb over, no bags there in sight.

"Tickets please", he calls out, looking only at me

"there's no need to shout " I think, gripping my tea.

He clips it just once in a flash he has gone

it's like magic I think as I'm once more alone

but no doubt there'll be others for him on the train

as he wanders the corridors searching in vain.

I look at my ticket punched through till it's torn

if it gets clipped again it will be more or less gone

but at least he was happy, his mission worthwhile

and I must say he did it with plenty of style.

Planning Ahead

Energy expended but in a fragmented way

my mind is full of ideas, plans, which tend to go astray.

Yet it all seems clear, so very clear, in the middle of the night

thoughts flood my brain and make me think this time I'll get it right.

But morning comes the office calls, no time to think them through

and before I know it they're pushed aside, there's so much else to do.

I really need some discipline, that's what I tell myself

to make the time to plan ahead, not leave plans on the shelf

for if I don't don't the days will pass and all my hopes and schemes

will be added to that growing list of long forgotten dreams.

Far From Home.

I sit here pensive, quietly, wondering what to do
feeling lost and far from home, so far away from you.
The night is long, minutes drag by endlessly
while outside the buzz seems alien, a world apart from
me.

The hours slip by, the room grows dark, as sunset finally
falls
it's fading light casts shadows on my hotel room walls.
The intermittent flicker of neon lights the room
yet strangely doesn't change the air of solitary gloom.

I rise and close the curtains and climb back into bed
and rub my eyes and stretch right out, lay down my
weary head.
Another town, a stranger, where no one knows my name
it's sadly one more part of the great big business game.

The Concert

What a night this had been

a resounding success

the wait was long but worth it

and boy did she impress.

The theatre's full but every word

it seems is meant for me

I sit transfixed, oblivious to all reality.

Some songs so sad they pierce my heart

I struggle to hold back tears

but then the spell is broken

as the next one fills my ears.

My mood so sad a moment ago

is suddenly transformed

and with the words of this lovely song

my aching heart is warmed.

She finishes her last song

it seems there'll be no more

but I join the cheering crowd

as we call for an encore.

She heeds our pleas

walks back on stage,

pleased by the crowds acclaim,

and sings one more so beautifully

we're absolutely drained.

And now at last it's over

she's gone, the audience leaves.

and I make my way back home again ,

music's such a sweet release.

One More Night

It's Sunday night,

behind me the club lights melt into the cold sharp winter night

and I smile with sheer contentment everything had gone just right.

Yet I had gone on stage before what seemed an apathetic crowd

wondering how the show would go, the band were far too loud.

"I'll have to work tonight" I thought, as the compere called my name

then walked on stage and smiled at them, and sang my first refrain.

My spirits lifted instantly, the band were really tight

some people smiled a welcome, could it really be alright?

Indeed my fears were groundless, I was at one with them around me

my early worries banished they seemed now unnecessary.

As I worked my way through my act, the atmosphere changed completely

the crowd were now exhilarated, clapping and cheering wildly.

I came offstage with their applause ringing in my ears

I felt so good, so powerful, no trace of previous fears.

To transform a crowd and a place like that brings a feeling of pure bliss

and if it stopped tomorrow it's one I'd surely miss.

When I think of all the shows I've done

and the satisfaction that they've brought me

I hope I've given something back

to those who have come to see me.

But now as I sit here in my car

I think of the day ahead

where I'll be that other man, in another life

who must earn his daily bread

On Stage

Tonight I'm the hero, applause fills the air
my last song is over, they do really care.
As I take my bow, my heart pounds with delight
what a feeling it is, a real special night.

I've sung songs that were happy and some that were sad
made them smile and then cry and go home feeling glad
but the emotion was wrung not just out of them
although on a high I'm now totally drained.

It's hard to explain how you feel at that time
a magical link between their hearts and mine.
but now it's all over I go back to my room
get changed and set off all alone as a rule.

I would like to have savoured that feeling much longer
but there's always tomorrow I smile and look forward.

I am a Singer

I am a singer, I have a voice

tonight's been fantastic, the room rings with applause.

They are calling my name "please just sing one more"

so I turn and head back from my dressing room door.

The band play the first chords, the house lights grow dim,

and the mood is created as I start to sing.

The words speak of passion, of longing, of love

as I pour out my heart, they just can't get enough.

To others they are words, to me the real thing,

and I'm lost in their meaning whenever I sing.

The feeling is sensual, and when I finish I'm drained

but they call me over and over again.

I come back for a bow and then leave the stage

the crowd are still cheering as I give them a wave.

I feel that they're taking a part of me home

so maybe for some then they won't be alone.

Dreams

Trapped and tired and feeling low
wondering where on earth to go
even walks lead nowhere new
just same old scenery, same old views.

Somehow I just can't find the time
to visit relatives of mine
friends neglected too it's sad
when I think of all the times we've had.

Those days of fun with ne'er a worry
but now life's all just hurry scurry
I have so much I want to do
and hope that God allows me to.

Though after work there's little chance

to plan ahead in life's fast dance

but one day soon I'll have the time

and put in place these dreams of mine

Lost Love

I watch her as she passes that sad look upon her face

then she smiles and all too quickly she's gone without a trace.

The smell of her sweet perfume lingers on for quite some time

and I'm captured by her beauty but she's no longer mine.

Still I'm with her in my thoughts and dreams in all my fantasies

but now that it's all over there's nothing left but tears.

I wish that I could hold her and tell her how I feel

but that may never happen all I have are memories.

Maybe someday things will change again and she'll come back to me

and tell me that she loves me oh how happy I would be.

I'd put my arms around her and hold her really tight

and promise that I'll always, always treat her right.

Green Fields

Green fields fringed by trees
with sleepy meadows, sparkling seas
these are my dreams of paradise
far away from the bustle of city life.

I'd love to live in a country town
with pleasant walks, time to slow right down.
I need the space and the open air
and I just can't function if they're not there.

The sense of freedom would be so sweet
the deadlines I no longer had to meet.
Am I anti- social? I can't agree
we're all made different you and me.

Contentment's important and we try hard to find it

and whilst it's sometimes elusive, the pursuit is worth it

but for now I'll go back to my work in the city

and do what's now become my duty.

An Evening Walk

It's half past ten should I go to bed or go out for a walk.

I settle for the latter and quickly grab my coat.

The air is sweet, delicious, it takes my breath away

the streets almost deserted, me the solitary stray.

Singing to myself I stroll along, oblivious to all around

myself my sole companion, the wind the only sound.

I choose the songs quite carefully, they have to match my mood

but tonight was not a problem, I was feeling really good.

I had almost sung an album as I got back to my gate

I'd better quieten down I thought as it was pretty late.

So with that thought fixed in my head I opened my front door,

I'd given a concert to the wind, but it didn't ask for more.

Relax

Do you ever sit and dream and think of what life's all about

some things aren't what they seem, of that there is no doubt.

Take a summer day in June when you are lying on the beach

you feel the whole world's at your feet but still there's something out of reach.

Walk along the coastal path, breathe that pure sea air

it'll help to clear your mind and to ease the burden there.

Try to dream instead of worry, there's no point in trying to hurry

the world will just go on anyway.

So save your thoughts for something real, tell your family how you feel

help the love to go around, make fun and laughter common sounds.

Think of those worse off than you in what they try to do

then your life will be worthwhile, so let's start it with a smile.

Daydream

Committee meetings, smoky rooms, just another day,

but sitting here if truth be known, I'm many miles away

to country lanes in sunny climes, where deadlines don't exist,

where life is meant for living, these thoughts I can't resist.

Holidays

The holidays are almost gone, the struggle looms ahead

and soon I'll have to leave this lovely village in the Med.

These last few days with not a care in the bliss that's Southern France,

have seemed unreal and magical, a pause in life's frenetic dance.

Instead of phones and constant stress the only sounds I've known

are those of nature at its best as I walk the shores alone

Yet it's strange to think that while I dream the other world goes on

and I can fit into them both like some uncharted pawn.

But I put the thoughts out of my mind as the sun begins to set

and lift my drink and settle back, there's still some time left yet.

We've won the cup!

Just 5 minutes to go, the scores were level pegging

we'd spurned far too many chance that had sadly gone a begging

but then in that final minute we'd had that bit of luck

the winning goal was scored and at last we had the cup.

All at once the crowd erupted in a sea of green and white

and when the whistle went for time well it was sheer delight.

Joy, relief, exhilaration, a feeling of pure bliss

but oh how different it would have been if Chalmers he had missed.

The cup was then presented to another massive roar

and I did my best to join in, though my voice was now no more.

The winning team were evident with their parade of happy grins

the chance they had finally taken masking all their early sins.

But at last it was all over so with the happy throng

I made my way out of the ground singing club song after song.

Gradually the crowds thinned out as we all made our way home

but it was strange to leave that teeming crowd to be suddenly on my own.

It was then I felt the tiredness start to seep into my bones

I felt as if I'd played the game as my limbs began to groan

but boy it sure was worth it, my team hadn't let me down

so smiling to myself I made my way back into town.

We are but a song .
(Story contains 34 Song titles)

It had been a **lovely day** and as we reached her home, I took her in my arms and realised **for the first time** just how much she meant to me.

Recently, no matter what I was doing, or where I was going, she was **always on my mind** and I wondered if perhaps she had the same **feelings** for me.

She looked especially **wonderful tonight**, and something told me that she is just as **crazy** about me as I am about her.

Yet, it seemed like only **yesterday** since our first **hello** and I was **amazed** at just how far we had **come together.**

*There are no **words** to explain **my love** for this beautiful **lady** and now I realise only too well how it feels **to love somebody** like her. I think of her **constantly, night and day. In dreams** too she is often by my side.*

*__"Baby it's cold outside"__ I said, as she stepped from the warmth of the car into the **still** night air.*
*I put my coat around her shoulders and held her close to Me **"Please stay** with me tonight **darling, let's spend the night together**.*
*"I can't "she said." If only my life were as simple as that but it's not. I so want to be with you, but you know as well as I do that **you can't always get what you want.***

*When you are away I **miss you like crazy**. You have no idea just how much you mean to me, and **everytime we say goodbye** it breaks my heart but I want you to know that I'll always be **right here waiting** for you"*

*As I walked her to her door, the light was still on in her vestibule casting a warm glow over the entrance. It was then I noticed that she was **crying.***

*"**Don't**" I said, holding her close. Let's just just leave it for tonight. **I don't want to talk about it** anymore just now.*

I kissed her gently on the lips and stroked the hair from her face feeling the wetness of her tears and the warmth of her face on mine.

*"**Go now**" I said. It's been a **perfect day** and one to remember. I'll call you tomorrow, and don't worry, I know this isn't **easy** but I'm sure **that love will find a way.***

*I waved to her as I got into my car. The **drive** home was a long one, but **this moment in time** was one I would always remember, and one where I realised just how strong **the power of love** could be.*

Two Worlds

Silver fish glide swiftly through the sparkling foam

while up above the birds survey the scene below.

The air is still on this cold winter morn

a landscape still to waken from the chill of dawn.

Yet two hours hence the calm will disappear

as people waken from there sleep

the village will once again resound with life

of fun and laughter, sometimes strife.

The thought occurs these are two different worlds

yet each possessing their own separate rules

the pre-dawn peace precludes the human race

who only see the country's other face.

But one cannot exist without the other

inextricably they're linked sister and brother.

and ne'er can e'er these two worlds meet

two different strands of life's intricate weave.

It's almost noon and with the warming sun

the air rings with the sound of children having fun.

Families relax, it seems all the world's at play

as we edge further into one more glorious day.

So let's sit back and thank God for it all

a world that never ceases to enthrall.

We take it all for granted more's the shame

when instead we should be thankful in His name.

Another Day

Another day has come and gone
we've done so many things
some planned, some just reactions
to the challenges life brings.

The lucky ones lead carefree lives
where all their dreams come true
their hopes and aspirations met
so much to see and do.

But others struggle constantly
weighed down with so much stress
their lives a constant battle
for a bit of happiness.

Yet at birth there's so much promise

for families such a happy time

but sadly for so many

talent withers on the vine.

If only life were fairer

there must be some other way

and the world it's wealth, resources

shared far more evenly.

war, poverty ,injustice

should all be cast aside

and concentrate more fully

on improving people's lives.

Will it ever happen

there's so much still to do

but the world would be a better place

not just for me --but you.

Rhyme or reason

I'm not averse to writing verse

it's one of life's great pleasures

to share with others thoughts and dreams

is something that I treasure.

Sometimes it seems they write themselves

the words just seem to flow

and with a steady rhythm of their own

the story starts to grow.

We're all such complex creatures

a mix of reason and emotion

of hopes and aspirations

plans we strive to put in motion.

Some will see the light of day

others wither on the vine

but they'll all contribute in their way

someplace, somewhere, sometime.

I've always been a dreamer

but dreamers change the world you know.

they search for what is beautiful

and encourage it to grow.

Poems play their part in this

and take these words of mine

enhance and give them added meaning

with the luxury of rhyme.

So I'll just keep on writing

till the words dry up and then

I'll look back on them fondly

till the spark ignites again.

Play with words

"It's wonderful, sensational,
A Tour de Force" they say.
the critics all outdo themselves
with praise for my new play.

"It's theatre at its best" says one
whilst others loved the themes
of fantasy, of pure intrigue,
of someone elses dreams.

I read them all with great delight
my work was not in vain
the hours I'd spent outlining thoughts
ideas I'd tried to frame.

The cast had played their part in this

they had brought my words to life

the tensions and the drama

the passion and the strife.

Performances that stunned the crowd

then brought them to their feet

I felt that I could weep with joy

my dream at last complete.

The long, long hours I'd spent on this

the many sleepless nights

had proved to be successful

we've got our name in lights.

There may never be another

this perhaps the only one

a successful one hit wonder

or has the story just begun.

Broken Dream

*I woke up really late today
I'd slept longer than I should
my head still full of cotton wool
that warm and hazy interlude
before consciousness asserts itself
and drags us from our dreams
to the reality of daily life
and all our plans and schemes.*

*I lay there stretching lazily
still in that warm cocoon.
Just a few minutes more and I'll hit the floor
the day had come too soon.*

A Taste of Italy

The holiday's been booked for months

now it's almost time to leave

for the Amalfi Coast, Sorrento

and the Bay of Napoli.

My hotel sits high upon a hill

looking out to sea

and out there in the distance

the lovely island of Capri.

The Amalfi Coast is stunning

a jewel in the Med they say

towns and villages rich in history

and none more famous than Pompeii.

Yet I've only seen these sights so far

on TV or on film

but when my plane sets down on Italian soil

my holiday will begin.

I'm counting off the days now

it just can't come too fast

a holiday to remember

and I'm going there at last.

La Belle France

I love France with all it's Gallic charm
I love it's joie de vivre
from northern towns to southern climes
there's so much to see and savour.

Paris, so chic and beautiful
the city of romance
with it's boulevards and treasures
it's style and elegance.

From Notre Dame to Sacre Coeur
it's wonders are so many
and rising tall above them all
Le Tour d'Eiffel stands tall and mighty.

But away from all the city sights
there is that other France
with it's traditions, culture, way of life
that never ceases to entrance.

A landscape rich and varied
sights that take the breath away
majestic mountains, studded coastlines
towns and cities steeped in history.

Inland France's rural charm
has it's own delights
stunning vistas, rolling farmland
star filled skies at night.

I feel a sense of empathy
when I go back to France
and an endless fascination
for the joys of this fine land.

I've sampled much of what there is

but I know there's so much more

and I hope it's not too long before

I set foot once more on it's shores.

Crème Brulée

A perfect end to a perfect day
the meal had been exquisite
the restaurant simply oozes class
can't wait for my next visit.

We'd picked a table by the fire
and whiled the night away
the food was simply beautiful
topped off with crème brulée.

We shared some stories
drank some wine bathed in the fire's warm glow
till then at last we'd had our fill
and it was time to go.

I often look back on that night

and the surprise I had in store

and when at last it was time to go

I called again for more.

The People's Choice

He'd worked at his art for all those years
to world wide acclaim but not from his peers
yet the paintings so stylish that sprung from his hands
are cherished and sought for in so many lands.

His colours are vibrant, the scenes tell a tale
where beauty, elegance and style still prevail.
He takes us to Cannes, to cafes to rooms
where fantasy, dreams and love are the rules.

And now he's in Glasgow, the gallery is thronged
with so many people they can't all be wrong.
The art world stay distant, but he doesn't care
the people that matter will always be there.

Memories of Jack Vettriano's Glasgow Exhibition 2014

The woman she longed to be

*She had heard so much about it
and here she was at last
people queuing eagerly
such a wide and varied cast.*

*Paintings hung on every wall
with scenes of love, romance
atmospheric, sensual,
she was totally entranced.*

*She stopped in front of one of them
it seemed to take her breath away
a scene of passion, mystery,
her own secret fantasy.*

Just then she wished that she could be

the woman on the wall

and step into the painting

she was totally enthralled.

But reality soon hit her

as it was time to go

so she kept her thoughts all to herself

no one would ever know.

At times she thinks back on that day

with a sad and wistful smile

and sees again that lady

it had all been so worthwhile.

Their Rock in life

Her life had not been easy
as she struggled day by day
to put food on the table
working hard to pay her way.

Her husband he was long since gone
leaving her to cope
with two boys, a baby on the way
and very little hope.

Her obligations there were many
her resources they were few
but despite the challenges she faced
she worked hard to see it through.

Small in stature, big in heart
the epitome of grit
luxuries few and far between
her children they came first.

She was like so many others
the real heroes in our lives
selfless, caring, loving,
real people with real lives.

Her name will never be in lights
but I'm sure she means much more
to those who know and love her
and the children she adored.

In time of need.

He worked long hours in a factory
she cleaned offices each day
working hard to make a living
on meagre rates of pay.

Their lives were never glamorous
high fliers they were not
but their personal pride and decency
ensured they'd give it all they'd got.

But one day he was injured
caused by a faulty guard on his machine
his arm was trapped, his fingers crushed
before he could be freed.

Although a long time union member
he was a critic like so many
and complained about them constantly
"they're not worth a single penny"

But at this time in his hour of need
they really played their part
taking up his case with management
he wouldn't know where to start.

He lost many, many, months off work
feeling angry and frustrated
but his union handled everything
and he was fully compensated.

So there's a lesson there for everyone
at times we all need help
to cope with those occasions
when we can't do it by ourselves.

Time to call it a Day

I woke up tired this morning
still groggy, half asleep
thinking wearily of the day ahead
the appointments I must keep.

I'd done this job for forty years
but it had finally taken its toll
my youth long since departed
and I suddenly felt old.

But as I struggled out of bed
I knew the time had come
to sever ties and look ahead
relax and have some fun.

I looked back on a long career

with far more highs than lows

proud of my involvement

but now the time was right to go.

I thought of places visited

of all that I'd achieved

the many people that I'd met

and the friendships I had weaved.

I know I'll miss the buzz of work

the banter and the fun

and a team who really worked so hard

for each and everyone.

My mind felt so much clearer

now the decision had been made

and I could see a bright new future

for the road that lay ahead.

Still there is some work to do

committments I must keep

some months of heavy workload

more nights of broken sleep.

But soon it will be over

and I'll be free at last

to carve myself a future

quite different from my past.

To rhyme or not to rhyme

Rhyming poetry's out of date
that's what some people say
ideas and thoughts curtailed by rhyme
are not what readers want today.

It's fine they say for greeting cards
or bits of whimsy here and there
but for anything more serious
you have to look elsewhere.

I'm afraid they've missed the point in this
and in the beauty that is rhyme
expressed so very vividly
by those in earlier times.

Shakespeare, Yeats and Tennyson
Wordsworth, Burns and Donne
their words so rich and eloquent
with a rhythm much like song.

So let's disregard the notion
that trends have any part to play
in what poetry is all about
as nothing's really changed today.

It's an expression of our thoughts and dreams
and in what we want to say
and it's many styles and genres
all contribute in their way.

ABOUT THE AUTHOR

James Millar lives in Scotland.

This is his first book of poetry.

James who is one of Scotland's top male vocalists is well known in the

cabaret field under his stage name of Paul French.

Visit his website at:

www.paulfrenchvocalist.co.uk

Printed in Great Britain
by Amazon